OIKOS
A Practical Approach to Family Evangelism

OIKOS

A Practical Approach to Family Evangelism

Ron Johnson   Joseph W. Hinkle
Charles M. Lowry

BROADMAN PRESS
Nashville, Tennessee

Contents

Preface

Today's family, more than ever before, is faced with two very clear choices. It can follow temptations the world has to offer and ultimately be dashed to pieces on the rocks of sin, or it can follow the will of God and, by so doing, gain stability as well as become the powerful force for evangelism that God intended the family to be.

Admittedly, we have not always looked deeply enough into the possibilities of the family as a force in evangelism. But with the renewed emphasis on the family today and with so many families in need of support from Christian families, the time is ripe to do so.

I was delighted when I saw the outline for this book. For the first time here is a resource in evangelism that is devoted to helping families realize their enormous potential and opportunity to be used of God in reaching a lost world.

God has richly blessed Southern Baptists by giving us many resources to utilize in reaching our world. We should use each one. *Oikos* evangelism is another resource that is waiting to be utilized. Think of the possibilities—one concerned Christian family burdened and committed to reach an entire lost family, to see each unsaved member of that family come to faith in Christ. If each Christian family in every Southern Baptist church would catch this vision, it could revolutionize our evangelistic efforts.

The real strength of this book lies not only in the way it looks at the Biblical basis for family evangelism and the need to do so but also in the practical projects it suggests for getting the job done. I am convinced that any pastor who wants to see his church mobilized in family evangelism can take this book and use it as a springboard to launch families into the practice of winning other families.

This book can be used not only by pastors, evangelism directors, and associational directors but by interested laymen who want to see others brought to Christ. The writers of this book lend strength and a variety of experiences to it. Let us who read it take every advantage from it.

C. B. Hogue
Director of Evangelism
Home Mission Board

Introduction

The pale yellow shadows of three strangers danced on the walls of Simon's house as oil lamps burned late into the night. Outside the sea waves filled the air with a pungent smell of fish. The fine sea mist carried the smells and the sounds of the Mediterranean through the open windows and into the tanner's house.

For several minutes Peter forgot the sea and the men who were guests in his friend's house. It was the vision. His mind replayed the events over and over again. The great sheet let down from heaven was filled with all kinds of animals and birds that he considered unclean.

His strict Jewish upbringing could not tolerate even the sight of such a collection. Yet his eyes focused on each creature. His hunger caused him to hear a voice, "Peter, here is food. Kill and eat." "No, no," came the voice of his upbringing. Then the other voice, much stronger and with more authority than the voices of his heritage, spoke again: "What God has made clean, you must not call unclean" (see Acts 10).

Three times he saw the great sheet. Three times the voices came. All day long he had been haunted by what the vision meant. His mind would not rest.

Once again Peter felt the strange urge that had

come over him during that experience. Earlier it had caused him to go down off the roof to meet the three men who now sat at the table with him. Now the strange feeling caused him to move beyond the vision, and he found himself listening once more to the men who spoke of Cornelius.

The strangers told again the story they had told Peter earlier in the day. Cornelius had prayed and a vision had come to him promising that his prayers were being answered. The angel had told Cornelius to send to Joppa where Peter would be found.

As they spoke of the vision of Cornelius, Peter again thought of his own vision. Could God have sent both visions? Could the vision of the forbidden animals have anything to do with carrying the gospel? Was it possible that God wished to pour out his Spirit on the Gentiles?

As weariness gave way to sleep, perhaps Peter dreamed of Pentecost. How wonderfully God had poured out his Spirit on those who believed. But little did Peter know that a new insight into God's redemptive work awaited him at Caesarea. He was about to see God at work in the lives of those he had not considered as candidates for eternal life. And Peter was about to experience not only the eagerness with which Cornelius wished to hear the gospel but also one of the most natural settings for sharing the message of God with another person.

Peter was able to share the message of salvation under what appeared as ideal circumstances. He shared the gospel in the small fellowship of Cornelius's home. Open, sincere, and informal discussion was possible.

There were no artificial barriers that separated Peter from his listeners. He stood with them. They could touch him, look him in the eye, and hear him clearly. He did not lecture to them but shared from his heart.

A climate of love and acceptance was possible because the ones who were assembled represented the household of Cornelius. Even Peter soon recognized the acceptance that was shown to him as Cornelius bowed before Peter.

When Peter preached and decisions were made, the household of Cornelius was transformed. There was no doubt that continued relationships of support, encouragement, and fellowship were made possible. This is the heart of *oikos* evangelism.

Oikos is a transliteration of the Greek word. In the New Testament *oikos* is used in several related ways. *Oikos* means house. It literally means a dwelling. Yet, as is the case with many Greek words, it means much more. It also carries the meaning of household or family. It can mean a whole household of people living together as a clan or in a tribe.

Hence, its broader meaning of household includes not only those persons who live in the house or under the same roof but also all of those persons who touch the household in terms of having a relationship to it. Immediate family members, extended family members, servants and their families, clients, and friends of the family would be part of the household or *oikos*.

The household was very important in New Testament days because it was woven into the fabric of the society. The family was the basic unit of the Roman society. Commerce, politics, religion, and influence were channeled through family ties. In fact, Michael Green says in his book, *Evangelism in the Early Church*, "The family understood this way, as consisting of blood relatives, clients and friends, was one of the bastions of Graeco-Roman society."[1]

It is easy to see how strategic the family was not only to the society of the day but also in the spread of religion. Green goes on to say, "Christian missionaries made a deliberate point of gaining whatever households they could as lighthouses, so to speak, from which the gospel could illuminate the surrounding darkness."[2]

Here then is the thesis of this book. Today the family can and must be an instrument through which the gospel reaches out into the world. No longer can families live to themselves, apart from a lost and dying world. Each family must seek to develop its own *oikos* to the extent that others in all areas of life are touched by it. *Oikos* evangelism is needed today.

1.
Biblical Foundations

Biblical Basis

When God stepped out into the darkness of space and time and spoke the universe into existence, he began a chain of events which would lead to his greatest creation, man. But even in paradise something was missing. So God made woman and thus designed forever the context in which human beings can live, the family.

A term for family in the Greek is the word *oikos*. Like many Greek words it carries a basic meaning and can be expanded to mean other things as well. *Oikos* has the basic meaning of house or dwelling. Its broader meaning, however, is that of household or family. It is this broader meaning that is important for this study of family evangelism.

Old Testament Backgrounds

The Old Testament reflects the Jewish understanding of the importance of family. The family served as the vehicle through which God's word was passed from generation to generation.

Although sin entered into the world and spoiled paradise, it did not spoil God's intention that man live in fellowship with him. Nor did it spoil God's intention that the family preserve and communicate the truths of God's word to itself and to others.

This *oikos* understanding of the family was based upon the Hebrew family group. Hans Walter Wolff, in *Anthropology of the Old Testament*, states that four generations generally belonged to the larger, patriarchal family group. It included the men, married women, unmarried daughters, slaves of both sexes, persons without citizenship, and "sojourners," or resident foreign workers.[3]

The Hebrew understanding of the family illustrates the larger context of the *oikos*. It not only included the blood relatives but it also reached out and touched persons from various walks in society.

It is interesting that in God's original promise to Abraham, as recorded in Genesis 12:1-3, families would be blessed as a result of God's plan. "And in you all the families of the earth shall be blessed." Obviously, this blessing had to do with God's will that man live in fellowship with him.

The family or household continued to play a significant role in the unfolding of God's salvation history. Wolff states that the family group, kindred, and the tribe were the most important components of ancient Israel's social structure.[4] When the families of Israel followed God's will, Israel's devotion to God did not suffer. Its religious commitment depended on the families and their commitment to God. Hence, God commanded each household to honor and follow the leadership of God.

"There also you and your household shall eat before the Lord your God and rejoice" (Deut. 12:7).

"And you shall rejoice before the Lord your God, you and your sons and daughters, your male and female servants, and the Levite who is within your gates" (Deut. 12:12).

"You shall eat in the presence of the Lord your God and rejoice, you and your household" (Deut. 14:26).

"These were the sons of Levi according to their fathers' households" (1 Chron. 23:24).

When Moses had completed the writing of the Law, he gave it to the priests and to all the elders of Israel along with specific instructions to gather together the entire larger *oikos* family to hear, learn, and observe it.

"Assemble the people, the men and the women and children and the alien ... in order that they may hear and learn and fear the Lord your God, and be careful to observe all the words of this law" (Deut. 31:12).

There are many examples in the Old Testament which illustrate the importance of the larger family or household. Even the sum of all the families, clans, and tribes—the entire nation—was called the "house of Israel" (2 Sam. 1:12).

New Testament Usage

Oikos, as used in the New Testament, continues the Old Testament tradition of including the larger family in its meaning. An almost ritual *oikos*-formula stressed the centrality of the household in Christian advance.[5]

"Her house" or "his house" was the regular term to indicate the members of one's family, including servants.[6] The apostolic church used the interlocking social systems of common kinship, community, and interest as the backbone for communicating the gospel.[7] Listed below are some of the Scriptures which illustrate the importance of the *oikos*.

Luke 8:39—The demoniac is told to return to his house and to describe what great things had happened to him.

Luke 19:9—Zacchaeus is told that salvation had come to his house that very day.

John 4:53—The royal official's son is healed. He himself believed and also his household.

Acts 10:2,24—Cornelius, who feared God with all his household, had a vision. He sent for Peter. When Peter arrived, Cornelius had gathered together his relatives and close friends.

Acts 16:15—Lydia responded to Paul's witness, and she and her household were baptized.

Acts 16:31—Paul told the Philippian jailer, "Believe in the Lord Jesus, and you shall be saved, you and your household."

Acts 18:8—Crispus, the leader of the synagogue at Corinth, believed in the Lord with all his household.

1 Corinthians 1:16—Paul baptized the household of Stephanas.

Hebrews 3:6—Christ was faithful over all his house, whose house we are.

1 Timothy 3:15—The household of God, which is the church of the living God.

There are also numerous references where the *oikos* principle is seen in action (family, household, friendship influence in evangelism) even though the word *oikos* is not used in the text.

Mark 2:14-15—Jesus called Matthew, the tax collector. Soon after there were many tax collectors dining with Jesus, and they were following him. Here is an example of the larger *oikos* extending to those who are linked by common interests.

Luke 5:18ff.—The lame man was brought to Jesus by his friends. Obviously, close friends cared for him. He was brought to Jesus by his *oikos*.

Luke 7:37 to 8:3—The sinful woman was forgiven, and soon other sinful women were brought to Jesus.

Each parable in Luke 15 illustrates the *oikos* principle.

Luke 15:1-8—The man found the lost sheep and called together his friends and neighbors, his *oikos*, to rejoice.

Luke 15:8-10—The woman found the coin and called together her friends and neighbors to rejoice.

Luke 15:11-32—The father called for rejoicing with friends when the lost son came home. The other son complained that he was never given opportunity to rejoice with his friends.

Luke 16:19ff.—Even the rich man in torment was concerned about his *oikos*—his five brothers who were lost.

John 1:40-41—Andrew brought his brother, Peter, to Christ.

John 1:44-45—Philip brought his friend, Nathaniel, to Christ. This is an example of friendship *oikos*.

John 4:9ff.—The woman at the well went into the city and told the people to come see the Messiah. This is an example of relationships in the *oikos* of the woman.

Modern Day *Oikos*

We have looked briefly at the Old Testament background for the *oikos* concept and the New Testament usage of the *oikos* principle. How then do we transfer this concept to the present?

Anthropological research indicates that there are worldwide units of society. These include the common kinship or the larger family consisting of blood relations, common communities or neighbors in the larger sense, common interests such as associates, work relationships, recreational acquaintances, avocations, and so forth. These social systems are not only relevant to life in our country but are also discernable in their own forms in other countries as well.

An *oikos* today might be described as a social system or a group of people related to each other through common ties and tasks.[8] Today, just as in the New Testament days, each person is very involved in his own *oikos.*

You can easily think of persons in your own *oikos* group. The illustration on page 19 shows the *oikos* that each person has. *Oikos* is not just a New Testament principle. It is very much at work in each person's individual world.

New Testament Churches

New Testament churches relied on the *oikos* of each person as one way to share the gospel. Large gatherings often were not possible because of persecution and other problems. Hence, the gospel message permeated the fabric of Graeco-Roman society through *oikos* relationships. It was the natural thing to do.

Several examples are seen in the New Testament. Cornelius, a man who worshiped God, wanted to share Peter's good news. He gathered his *oikos* and awaited Peter's arrival. At Peter's preaching the entire *oikos* of

OIKOS PRINCIPLE

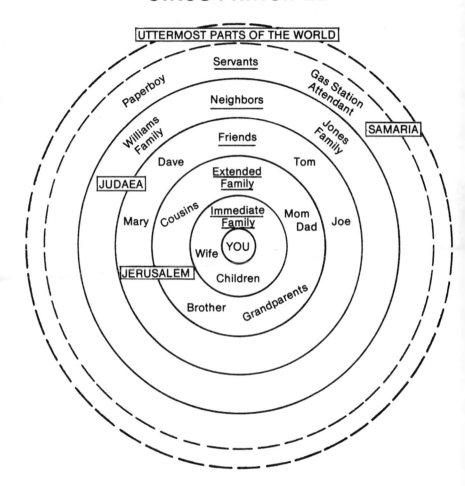

Design your own *Oikos* system. Write in the names of those who make up your *Oikos*.

This chart adapted from W. Oscar Thompson, Jr., *Concentric Circles of Concern* (Nashville: Broadman Press, 1981), p. 21.

Cornelius received the gospel and the Holy Spirit (see Acts 10:44).

The Philippian jailer received spiritual life and also extended physical life due to Paul's testimony. The jailer took the prisoners home with him to share Paul's message with his family (see Acts 16:29-33).

Even Andrew could not wait to tell his brother about the Messiah. Philip told his friend. On and on the gospel was carried (see John 1:35-49).

Today it is just as natural to share the gospel through *oikos* evangelism. A number of years ago a member of a gospel quartet was witnessing to a young Indian in Siloam Springs, Arkansas. He extended his hand in a warm handclasp acknowledging that he was accepting Jesus as his Savior. Then he abruptly left the gathering in the park and headed for town. Many wondered where he was going and even whether he was sincere in his profession of Christ. But in less than ten minutes he returned, out of breath, with a younger Indian lad. "Will you tell my brother about Jesus, too?" he asked. It was and is the natural thing to do. *Oikos* evangelism is the natural God-given means for sharing our supernatural message.[9]

New Testament churches relied on *oikos* evangelism also because it was the effective thing to do. In house after house, in small groups, family member to family member, friend to friend, worker to fellow worker, the gospel was spread. In informal settings, in a relaxed atmosphere, and in a caring climate, open discussion and real interchange of views could take place.

Large public meetings might have been dangerous. But house meetings, chance conversations, and family gatherings were an effective means of communicating the gospel. Modern missionary movements are spreading today in much the same way they did in New Testament days.

The *oikos* support system was equally important. When a person steps out of a non-Christian, uninterested, or even antagonistic background and accepts Jesus as Savior, a support, encouragement, and nurture system is helpful.

As others in the immediate *oikos* are influenced and won, a colony is established. As still others are won, a caring fellowship or *koinonia* group is established for strength and mutual support. The chances of continued discipleship and Christian growth are greatly enhanced.

Missionaries can relate dozens of stories where families who have been won together have been able to begin permanent productive churches in difficult, even hostile surroundings. Winning others within the *oikos* enhances survival and growth.

Religious Context of the Family

Marriage and family are not purely secular institutions. Any serious study of the Bible reveals that in both its origin and its later development, the family has basically a religious context. In his book, *Family Relationships and the Church*,[10] Oscar Feucht points out that the term "one flesh" in Genesis 2:24 encompasses not only the marital union of the man and woman, but also the family which results from that union, and that the term *basar* which is the Hebrew word for flesh was frequently used idiomatically to express family or blood relationships.

The family, understood in this way, becoming one flesh, being fruitful and multiplying, is seen as an ordinance of God, established by his creative will and act and not merely by a cultural phenomenon. The family became so basic that in Joshua 7:14 the entire nation was organized as a large "family of families." They came forward tribe by tribe, clan by clan, and family by family. So much is included in the Old Testament about families, that one writer states: "The Bible covers the subject of the family more thoroughly than any other ancient book on record."[11]

The New Testament continues this thorough emphasis on the family, its religious context, and its mission. The church and home are not seen as two distinctly separate institutions.

In Ephesians 5:21 to 6:4 the ideal family relationships are compared to the relationship between Christ and his church. Christ's love for the church is the standard for self-giving, unselfish love in the family. It is also the basis for husband-wife relationships in mutual submission to one another. It is done "in the fear [reverence] of Christ" (Eph. 5:21).

In Christ the family ideally expresses its mission. What is its mission? Though many duties are either stated or implied in the Bible, they seem to fall into three major categories: (1) family worship, (2) religious education, and (3) evangelism.

Family Worship

It is interesting to note that most of the significant celebrations and commemorations in Hebrew life were designed for family participation. Exodus 12:21-27 says, in the instructions for the Passover, "Select the animals for your families" (Ex. 12:21, NIV). Each family was to have a lamb. It was to be "a lasting ordinance for you and your descendants" (Ex. 21:24, NIV). The children were to participate. Fathers were instructed, "When your children ask you, 'What does this ceremony mean?' then tell them" (Ex. 21:26-27, NIV). When we recall that there were no synagogues at this time to perform this function, we see all the more the importance of the family in the observance.

Much of the family worship in patriarchal times was centered around the altar, giving credence to the popular "family altar" description of family worship. These altars and the celebrations and commemorations observed at them were a means whereby God-centered families passed their traditions, truths, history, and devotion from parents to children, generation after generation.

Edith Deen recalls the altars at Shechem, Bethel, Hebron, Moriah, Beersheba, and other places when she says, "It is no wonder that they, moving together from one altar to another, were recognized as a people of destiny, who had God-centered goals, and who moved steadfastly toward them."[12] Families today who have God-centered goals have a better chance of staying together, staying in love, and staying on target toward achieving those goals if they have regular family worship.

Although we do not observe the great festival occasions of the Hebrews, we can learn from their practice. Many of the same values from family worship can be achieved by us.

Oscar Feucht says that families which have worship together in the home gain at least eight benefits.[13]

1. Learn to know the Bible—Daily Bible reading gives a firsthand familiarity with the Bible that is attainable through no other way.

2. Face life with God—Families are able to have a message from God to live each day. They have a better sense of his will for the day.

3. Grow in reverence and prayer—Families learn what it is to hear one another pray. A sense of companionship through prayer is developed.

4. Spiritually trained children—Children grow up in the knowledge of God and have a background that prepares them to live in fellowship with God all through life.

5. Religion ceases to be a Sunday affair only—Religious awareness is expressed all through the week. Families learn to talk openly, casually, informally, and often about God.

6. The church is strengthened—Families who worship together each day form the backbone of the church. The influence of the church is extended into the world and Christian leaders are developed.

7. Christian citizens are developed—Good citizenship and Christianity are not enemies. Christians who are serious about God want to see a society in harmony with God's will.

8. A unified and enriched home—When families worship together, disharmony, tension, and distrust fades and does not surface as often.

Family worship procedure varies greatly among families. Some simply read a selected Bible passage and then pray. Others incorporate other elements, extending sometimes even to a special place or room arranged for family worship. There are some common elements that often surface in family worship:

Music—Some families sing a hymn or chorus; others simply read or quote a stanza of a favorite hymn.

Scripture—Some families read at random; many

will use a suggested plan such as those found in Sunday School materials, family magazines such as *Home Life* or *Open Windows*, or devotional books.

Devotional Comments—Some resources contain a brief illustration, story, or testimony relating to the Scripture reading of the day.

Discussion—Many families talk about the meaning of the passage that has been read. Family problems, opportunities, and plans often surface in these conversations.

Prayer—Fathers or mothers might lead in prayer. In some families, members alternate with each person taking the responsibility of prayer. Many families use sentence prayers while others use conversational prayers.

In his book, *One Home Under God,*[14] Jack Taylor pays tribute to the contribution of family worship to his own family and others during his ministry. Taylor lists several steps to beginning a family altar:

Be convicted of the absolute necessity for it.
Get the family together and discuss it.
Agree on a time and place.
Begin.

He suggests that it be continued in a planned fashion. It should be brief and biblical. It should involve the whole family, be serious but informal, interesting and varied, and not "preachy or chiding."

The first few times may seem a little awkward, but with a positive, informal, committed, continuing effort, family worship will not only become comfortable but it will also make a lasting, valuable contribution to the lives of family members. Pauline and Elton Trueblood said, "If we can believe that the home is potentially a sanctuary, we are well on our way to the recovery of family life."

Religious Education

In the early days of Israel's life there were so synagogues, no church schools, and no Sunday Schools. Religious education was totally the responsibility of the family. Even after the introduction of these institutions into religious life, the family remained primarily responsible with the church assisting. This was true even in the first several hundred years of the church.[15] The practice of almost completely turning over the religious education of children to the church is of relatively recent origin.

Evidence indicates that this shift of responsibility created a situation that is not as effective as the home-primary and church-assisting practice. One of the key findings of the study, *Religion in America, 1979-80*,[16] deals with "unchurched Americans." The sharpest difference in the background of the churched and unchurched related to "instruction by parents at home." Although the number of churched and unchurched who had experienced Sunday School and/or religion courses in school was almost exactly the same, the unchurched reported forty percent less "instruction" by parents at home.

Religious Education in the Old Testament

Religious education in the Old Testament home was very positively commanded and regularly emphasized. It was not so much a segmentized or separate function of the family as it was "functionalized," related to everyday happenings and activities at home. Walter Wegner states, "In short, it was to be nurture of persons, so that sons and daughters — by situational, relational, and formal teaching in the family — might grow up spiritually, mentally, socially, and physically."[17] His statement reminds us of the growth pattern of the young Jesus in his home (see Luke 2:40, 52).

This "life-style teaching" is most clearly commanded in Deuteronomy 11:19: "Teach them [the Commandments] to your children, talking about them when you sit at home, and when you walk along the road, when you lie down and when you get up" (NIV). The teaching was to be very open and intentionally done, not only in hearts and minds, but with symbols and ornaments worn on their hands and foreheads, and even written on door frames and gates.

Even length of life and residence in the land were related to such religious education in the home. "So that your days and the days of your children may be many" (Deut. 11:21, NIV). In many other passages, home and family religious education is emphasized:

Exodus 13:1-14 — (the ceremony of the consecration of the firstborn) "In days to come, when your son asks you, 'What does this mean?' say to him ... " (Ex. 13:14, NIV).

Joshua 4:1-24 — (crossing of the Jordan and twelve stones piled up) "In the future, when your children ask you, 'What do these stones mean?' tell them" (Josh. 4:6-7, NIV).

Deuteronomy 4:9 instructs the people, "Do not forget the things your eyes have seen or let them slip from your heart as long as you live. Teach them to your children and to their children after them" (NIV).

There were times when public instruction was to be

given also. "Assemble the people—men, women and children, and the aliens [sojourners or strangers] living in your towns—so they can listen and learn to fear [reverence] the Lord your God and follow carefully all the words of this law" (Deut. 31:12, NIV). Nevertheless, the predominant commands and practices were related to instruction in the family and home.

New Testament

This emphasis on family purpose and practice is continued in the New Testament. Fathers are urged to "bring them [children] up in the discipline and instruction of the Lord" (Eph. 6:4). Paul pointed out that from early childhood Timothy had been familiar with the sacred writings which have power to lead to salvation through faith in Jesus Christ. Timothy's faith was traced through Lois, his grandmother, and Eunice, his mother (see 2 Tim. 1:5; 3:15). He is an excellent example of what can be achieved through serious religious instruction in the home.

How different is this biblical example and instruction from so many situations today where religious instruction is rarely done in the home! Paul Vieth says that we profess to advocate the priesthood of believers; yet, so far as religious education is concerned, we have turned over the child to a "priesthood of teacher specialists."[18]

To be biblical, to be effective, and to recover the basic purposes of the home, we must educate and involve parents in religious education in the family. The church cannot do it alone; nor can the home do it alone; both, working together as a team, can achieve it most successfully.

Mark Short tells about being attacked by a black-capped chickadee. Bird lovers will recognize this as one of the smallest of birds, far smaller than a sparrow. Mark saw and heard this bird fussing at him from a low limb of a tree. He walked over, not noticing that he was also getting close to a fence post with a small hole in it. As he approached, the chickadee chirped furiously and dived at him, actually hitting him on the shoulder. As he retreated, a second chickadee emerged from the hole in the fence post. As Mark retreated (whether from fear or from respect for the cute, fiesty birds, we'll never know), he could not help but be impressed with the courage and determination of the chickadees to protect their home and family at all costs, against all comers. Religious education, family instruction in the home, greatly enhances the ability of your home to nurture, guide, and lead your children to salvation and the ultimate purposes of God in their lives. If the chickadees care that much for their young, surely we should have the same kind of concern for our families.

Evangelism

Where do we place evangelism in the mission of the family? It is the prime objective toward which family worship and religious education point and build.

A word study of the Great Commission, Matthew 28:19-20, clearly reveals that making disciples is the imperative, the ultimate goal around which the participles of "going, baptizing, and teaching to observe" revolve. Studies of family-related Scriptures reveal the same ultimate goal and objective; though it is also clear, as in the passage in Matthew, that nurture and continued instruction must continue beyond the initial experience of salvation.

Therefore, it seems appropriate to place evangelism as the ultimate objective of the family and home relationships. This is especially true if we view evangelism as far more than an initial conversion experience. Nurture and growing up into Christ are very much at the heart of evangelism and the family.

Paul told Timothy that his early childhood education in the sacred writings had power to lead him "to salvation through faith in Jesus Christ" (2 Tim. 3:15). This concept is clearly emphasized in the Old Testament also. In Psalm 78:1-8, parents sang that they would not hide from their children the parables and "things hidden from of old" (Ps. 78:2, NIV). They would show to the generation to come the praises of the Lord, his strength, and his wonderful works. They remembered that they had to make the Lord's way known to their children. They did this so that the generation to come might know the Lord's way. Children yet to be born would tell their children and so on from generation to generation.

Why would they do all this? In order that "they would put their trust in God and would not forget his deeds but would keep his commands" (Ps. 78:7, NIV). This was the mission. It was the ultimate objective.

It was so intended from the beginning of God's dealings with the family. Theologians speak of "salvation history" as they trace the work and plan of God from Abraham, through whose offspring or descendants all families of the earth were to be blessed (Gen. 12:3), to the culmination in Jesus Christ, the son of Abraham. (See Matt. 1:1-17; Luke 3:23-38; Acts 3:25; Rom. 4:16; Gal. 3:8.) Wegner says, "These New Testament texts continue the approach of the Old Testament, setting the giving, the renewal, and the eventual fulfillment of the divine promises to Abraham into the context of marriage and the family."[19] It extended through the Old Testament, through the New Testament, and even to today.

The family was central in God's "salvation history," and clearly is still related, still a major channel in the transmission of faith from generation to generation. It is still effective in true evangelism of spouse, children, parents, and the extended family or *oikos*.

Paul even encouraged the Christian mates of unsaved persons to stay with them for the sake of the children. In 1 Corinthians 7:12-16, he seems to be saying that, ritualistically, the cleanness of the believer overpowers the uncleanness of the unbeliever, allowing the relationship to continue, in the hope that the unsaved member may be influenced toward salvation.

Jesus was very clear in his response to the disciples' rebuke of the mothers who were bringing their children to him. A correct, modern speech translation of his response would be, "Let the children come to me. Stop stopping them" (Mark 10:14). His tenderness and concern were evident as he took the children in his arms, put his hands on them, and blessed them.

Jesus is still interested in receiving little children unto himself. What a beautiful experience it must have been for those mothers who brought their children to Jesus! It is just as beautiful today.

The Situation Today

There are forces at work today which adversely affect family living and create a critical need for *oikos* evangelism. The examples listed below are only a representation of the situation.

1. The large numbers of unsaved youth and adults

in *oikos* groups today. It is alarming to discover the large numbers of unsaved youth who make up the Sunday School rolls. Many of these youth are from Christian families. Perhaps little effort has been made to reach them for Christ.

A reemphasis on *oikos* evangelism, leading our own children to Christ, is needed. As an example, the following chart shows baptisms and Sunday School enrollment in age groups for the Southern Baptist Convention. Is it safe to assume that each person enrolled in Sunday School already has made a profession of faith?

2. The large number of youth dropouts and youth/parent "generation-gap" problems. Many parents have lost the sense of privilege and responsibility for helping their own children develop and grow in all areas of their lives. An emphasis on the family *oikos* responsibility could help heighten awareness and effectiveness in this problem area.

Lutheran Youth Research, an office for research and statistical analysis among Lutheran young people, discovered that the highest factor influencing the involvement or lack of involvement of youth in church was the personal involvement of the parents.[20]

Parents' responsibilities to their own children are more than teaching them table manners, how to tie their shoes, how to ride a bicycle, or how to choose a vocation. It includes life's most important and wonderful choice, Jesus Christ as personal Savior. Parents who are personally involved in leading their children to Jesus Christ develop a relationship base which enhances all other future relationships with their children.

3. Uncertainty and confusion created by propaganda, modern day cults, isms, and questionable evange-

BAPTISMS
1980

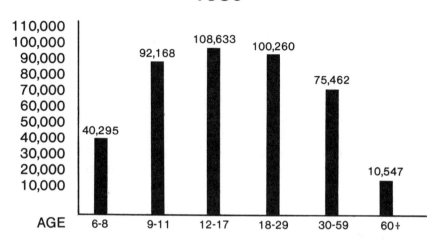

SUNDAY SCHOOL
TOTAL ENROLLMENT BY
AGE GROUPINGS
1980

6-11	12-17	18-29	30-59	60+
1,238,331	1,142,807	1,173,624	1,778,396	1,001,023

Figures from *The Quarterly Review,* July, August, September 1981, pp. 21, 32.

lism methods with children. Many parents and church leaders are rightfully concerned about the influences these groups are having on children and youth. What better way to offset them than to help parents learn how to win their primary *oikos*—their own children, learn how to establish a spiritual support group right there in their own *oikos*, and then learn to be a regular part of the *oikos* of God which is the church. Parents who lead their children to Christ can watch over their spiritual development and put to rest some of the false doctrines that may crop up during the growing years.

4. The rootless nature of life today. Many families move about so much that it is difficult to establish support groups or strong *oikos* relationships. Many have few close friends. The secularized, depersonalized, fast pace of life today has caused many people to retreat into a shell or lose hope of finding meaningful relationships.

Recent studies in personal relationships have revealed that the average person today has regular contact with about eighty persons. These contacts, properly cultivated, intentionally warmed up, and positively influenced, could be a great *oikos* resource. It is hard to imagine the total number of persons included in the *oikos* relationships of the members of the average church.

In a world where people need and long for friendship, companionship, a caring fellowship, and mutual support—where they are too wrapped up in the tangible to cultivate the spiritual, and too skeptical and afraid to reach out for help—there is a real need and opportunity for a reawakening of the Christian *oikos*, the family of God.

The Christian *oikos* faces a real challenge to become

aware of the *oikos* relationships each Christian has and to promote conditions and programs which will help each person reach out and witness to *oikos* members, leading them to faith in Jesus Christ and involvement in God's *oikos,* his church.

2.

Creating a Climate for *Oikos* Evangelism

Oikos evangelism depends on the climate that exists within the home of those who would seek to be evangelists. A healthy spiritual, personal, and social climate within family relationships is essential. Families in *oikos* evangelism share Christ out of the depth of their own spiritual resources. Their spiritual resources come from their daily communion with Christ and their applied knowledge of the Bible.

A sense of inadequate spiritual resources will naturally hinder a family from becoming involved with others. If the daily activities of some of the family members are not in harmony with Christian conduct, it is doubtful whether a family will be eager to do *oikos* evangelism.

The status of relationships among family members themselves is of utmost importance. If there are major unresolved conflicts between husband and wife, parents and children, or children and other children, it will be extremely difficult for a family to be effective with others. Spiritual commitment, personal purity, and harmonious relationships are essential elements for developing a climate for involvement.

The major question, therefore, is how does a

family build a climate for effective *oikos* evangelism?
It happens in at least four ways:

1. Nurture Christian values in daily life-style.
2. Affirm the vast potential of each family
   member.
3. Carefully meet one another's needs.
4. Accept God's presence.

Nurture Christian Values

In the course of living each day, a growing Christian family learns to nurture the values of personal faith. A Christian life-style reflects the true commitment of a family to the lordship of Christ. This commitment directs the family in its daily activities, influences attitudes, and governs the use of God-given resources.

The constant presence of the living Lord in their midst gives each member of the family a unique feeling of personal security. The abiding presence of the Holy Spirit within the believer fulfills a precious promise of Jesus (John 14:16).

The presence of Christ permeates the daily experiences of Christian family members. Their life-style reflects the reality of that presence in the gatherings of the family. His presence constantly reassures each family member of the strong bond of love that strengthens every fiber of their relationship.

Daily stresses, regardless of the nature of the stress and source, naturally dilute themselves as they blend into the settling peace furnished by the abiding presence of the Holy Spirit. This reality, when acknowledged and appropriated into the normal flow of daily family living, becomes a vital ingredient in building an ideal climate for *oikos* evangelism.

The family dedicated to the call of Jesus vigorously embraces those eternal principles set forth by Christ himself. Family members who have accepted Jesus as the Lord of their lives joyfully seek to understand God's will and walk in his ways.

They realize their shortcomings and call upon the grace of the Lord to forgive their daily sins and free them from the corrosive effects of guilt. They gladly affirm the challenge of Jesus to "be perfect, as your heavenly Father is perfect" (Matt. 5:48). Furthermore, born-again family members heartily commit themselves to live out the principles of Jesus' teachings. Daily walking in God's will and joyfully following his principles add other strong fibers to the total fabric of the ideal family climate for *oikos* evangelism.

Family members who stay acutely aware of God's guiding purpose for their lives consistently nurture those spiritual values which demonstrate a Christian life-style. The need for intimate spiritual fellowship with the Lord and the desire to please him come from the stabilizing knowledge of his purposes for Christian family living.

To be in step with his purposes brings congeniality to family relationships, even in face of enormously difficult circumstances. Furthermore, personal commitment to the purpose of the Lord for the family becomes a solid stage on which each member can stand together facing and resolving conflict.

When family members embrace an identical purpose for daily living and future direction, together they can find personal, satisfying, and fulfilling solutions to any conflict situation. Thus the family's daily involvement in fulfilling the guiding purpose of the Lord in its living adds yet another strong fiber to the total fabric of the ideal climate for *oikos* evangelism.

No family has within itself the power to accomplish these worthy purposes and live out these lofty ideals. Therefore, the family dedicated to "grow to the measure of the stature of the fulness of Christ" (Eph. 4:13, RSV) in its daily life-style relies on the enabling strength of the Holy Spirit. The Holy Spirit clearly enables family members to know and experience "what no eye has seen, nor ear heard, nor the heart of man conceived, what God has prepared for those who love him" (1 Cor. 2:9, RSV).

The Holy Spirit, unseen and unknown by the unsaved, dwells within each believer. He teaches him all things and guides him into all truth. The urging of the Holy Spirit is there to provide the impetus for witnessing to the lost.

The work of the Spirit in the inner man bestows freedom and produces the fruits of love, joy, peace, patience, kindness, goodness, faithfulness, gentleness, and self-control (see Gal. 5:22-24). The active work of the Holy Spirit frees family members from a life of self-conceit, provocation of one another, and envy of one another (see Gal. 5:26). The power of the Holy Spirit living within family members adds another strong fiber to the total fabric of the ideal climate for *oikos* evangelism.

Affirm Personal Potential

God granted vast potential to the human family when he "created man in His own image ... male and female He created them" (Gen. 1:27). In addition,

"God blessed them, and God said to them, 'Be fruitful and multiply, and fill the earth, and subdue it; and
rule over the fish of the sea and over the birds of the
sky, and over every living thing that moves on the
earth' " (Gen. 1:28). God gave persons stewardship
responsibilities with regard to his creation.

God granted a uniqueness to persons when he
"breathed into his nostrils the breath of life; and man
became a living being" (Gen. 2:7). God gave persons
the unequaled capacity to develop satisfying or dis-
appointing relationships with God and with one
another. In addition, God freely gave man the unique
gift for doing that which pleased or displeased God
and others.

Vast potential is inherently implanted into the
nature of man because he is created in the image of
God. Family members need to acknowledge and
affirm this reality in one another. Affirmation of that
uniqueness enables family members to utilize the
strength of it in daily living. Living awareness of the
God-given gift of personal potential affects and enhances the climate for *oikos* evangelism.

God's depth of being in man affirms the vast
potential of family members. Those who live in the
light of this reality never grow weary of one another
and cast one another aside as insignificant and
unworthy. Rather, they are constantly amazed at the
beautiful, interesting, and exciting insights they discover about one another.

The diverse gifts which emerge among family
members reveal another dimension of personal
potential. The diversity of gifts, abilities, and prefer-
ences among family members makes possible a var-

ied and exciting unity in family living. As in the church family, every family member does not have identical gifts. Neither should family members covet or be jealous of the gifts of another family member. They should affirm, appreciate, and encourage full utilization of individual gifts for the honor and glory of Christ (see 1 Cor. 12:12-31). As Paul challenged Christians earnestly to desire the higher gifts, so family members should challenge one another to desire the more excellent gifts.

The most excellent gift of all, and the one within the ability of all to achieve and use lavishly, is the gift of love. When the gift of love finds creative outlets within family relationships, its positive effects radiate beyond that of the family unit to others (see 1 Cor. 13:1-13).

As family members discover, affirm, and use their gifts for God, they find courage to witness to new acquaintances. After much trial and many errors in their witnessing, they will come to believe, "I can do all things through him who strengthens me" (Phil. 4:13).

This fundamental reality of Christian privilege not only emphasizes the struggle to do God's work, but it also affirms the potential of each individual. The courage to venture acknowledges the truth that says, "Not that I have already obtained this or am already perfect; but I press on to make it my own, because Christ Jesus has made me his own ... but one thing I do, forgetting what lies behind and straining forward to what lies ahead, I press on toward the goal for the prize of the upward call of God in Christ Jesus" (Phil. 3:12-14, RSV).

The spirit of loving persistence permits the life-style of the family to become involved in *oikos* evangelism. Grateful attention and affirmation of the vast potential of each family member are other strong fibers in the fabric of the ideal climate for *oikos* evangelism.

Meet Family Needs

Unmet personal needs hinder spiritual growth within the family. Family members who live on a starvation diet of love, affirmation, acceptance, appreciation, the need to be needed, feelings of being important to one another, and commitment to one another find it impossible to get excited about evangelism of other families.

Who can give to others out of an empty vessel? Families living at the poverty level of meeting one another's needs must allow their charity to begin at home. Spiritual poverty plagues scores of Christian families today. They feel spiritually defeated, morally beaten, and aimless in their direction. That kind of situation calls for a new beginning with one another.

Each day on the Christian pilgrimage requires fresh repentance, renewed commitment, discipline, and excitement on the part of the disciple. Likewise, family members can make new beginnings with one another and restore the joy of living together. Personal and spiritual renewal will open up streams of new vitality into daily living as family members commit themselves to care for and meet one another's needs to be loved, appreciated, affirmed, accepted, needed, and to feel important.

Family members know they are loved and appreciated when they hear it. They feel even more appreciated when they see it expressed by other family members. Five of the most important words in any language are, "I love and appreciate you."

Every member of the family needs to hear these powerful words every day. Think of the most loving thing you can imagine and do it to every member of your family. Make a personal list of every member of your family and write out beside each name what you are going to say and do to meet that person's needs. Slowly and surely the entire family will be transformed from a spiritually and emotionally starved and deprived condition to persons who are filled with life and joy. Families who daily work together at caring for and meeting one another's personal and spiritual needs have enormous reserves to share with other families in the community.

Daily personal and spiritual renewal requires quality time together. Busy families must decide upon their priorities and set aside prime time together for prayer and Bible reading, sharing with one another, giving and receiving support from one another, and making sure that everyone truly knows how very important each one is to the others.

In addition, individual family members should be sensitive to those times for giving spontaneously a meaningful word or physical expression to show loving care. This kind of loving behavior drives away negative attitudes, feelings, and behavior from family relationships. When this kind of caring consistently displays itself, the truth is spoken in love.

Family members do not need to stay on a spiritual and emotional high in order to meet one another's needs. Families who try this find that they soon become drained and revert to old threadbare spiritual and emotional poverty. This kind of whiz-bang attempt to meet one another's needs will very likely end in dismal failure. Then families are reluctant to try new beginnings. They may choose to live at the base line of their existence and drift aimlessly along with each person suffering in his own indifference.

The approach which wears well for every family member is the consistent, committed approach which calmly involves one another in what is going on within the family. This approach encourages open communication among family members in which the family sets priorities, plans activities together, and everyone works at being a diversified unit.

This style of meeting needs is similar to a family that has consistent mealtimes in which hungry appetites are satisfied. Everyone can count on mealtime and look forward to the satisfying effects it brings. A family committed to meeting one another's needs will be consistent and regular, and satisfaction will be assured.

Meaningful family rituals will emerge as time goes by. Some of these rituals will become a part of daily routine. Others will be seasonable in nature. Some families choose to keep a Bible on or near the dining table. They regularly read from it, discuss its meaning, and have prayer together following the evening meal. This prime time together gives the family members opportunity to express their loving care to one another personally and in prayer.

Another meaningful ritual may be the standard practice of kissing family members as each one departs for work, school, and so on. A hug, kiss, and "I love you," sends them away knowing they are loved and appreciated. Whatever the day might bring in the form of blessings or heartaches, family members have the assurance of love and appreciation. As family members return home for the evening, the ritual is repeated. Each member knows he is welcome at home and that he is loved and appreciated. Always remember that this loving behavior is meeting important needs.

Seasonal rituals also take on special meaning as years go by. Some families traditionally read the Christmas story from the Bible on Christmas morning before the presents are opened. Also, the Christmas stockings hanging on the fireplace mantle have special significance and are all a part of special times together. Families enjoy special Thanksgiving, Labor Day, and Independence Day activities for expressing loving behavior. Special tribute, honor, and praise should be showered upon individual family members on their birthdays, anniversaries, graduations, and so on. Creative use of special occasions consistently reminds family members that they are loved and appreciated.

Expressions of loving warmth stay in the mind and heart. Remembering some of the most special loving moments assures individuals that they are needed, wanted, and important.

The Lord knows we have needs, He encourages us to ask that they be met (see Matt. 7:7-12). The Lord knows that strength is renewed and ministry can be provided when our needs are met. God the Father met every need of the Son, even giving him strength to bear the sins of the world on the cross. He promises to meet our need (see Phil. 4:19). God the Father renews strength as needed (see Isa. 40:28-31). Meeting one another's needs is a vital fiber in the total fabric of the ideal climate for *oikos* evangelism.

Accept God's Presence

Accepting life's unfolding experiences, good and bad, requires a simple faith firmly established in God. Accepting life in its beauty and ugliness, serenity and turmoil, health and illness, affluence and need, living and dying is a major step for personal and spiritual fulfillment for the family.

Christian families know they honor Christ as they accept life's unfolding events with a deep sense of God's presence, peace, and good humor. Families who develop the will and disposition for *oikos* evangelism lay aside resentment, jealousy, greed, selfishness, and malcontent. In the place of these corrosive and divisive attitudes of spirit, they have added a joyful zest for life and peaceful contentment.

Their family life-style reflects that contentment in Christ. They blend family discipline and enthusiasm together. Their commitment to the lordship of Christ sets their perimeters for family behavior. Family discipline is the process of learning and living consistently in the lordship of Christ. This spiritual attitude within the family provides freedom to experience abundant life in all situations and circumstances.

Family discipline is the process by which a family becomes what it is meant to be in the will and purpose of God. This disciplined approach to life provides adequate flexibility for life planning and decision making. A disciplined family life-style provides the internal strength for the family to accept and work through the unexpected traumas of life, and to embrace unexpected opportunities as they reveal themselves.

Necessary and normal changes in family living do not threaten nor defeat basic purposes, but rather change should stimulate growth and enhance personal and spiritual fulfillment. Disciplined living in Christ enables families to establish worthy lifelong priorities which they understand and accept as the will of God for them. They rest, knowing the presence of God leads them. The lordship of Christ is clearly seen in their past experiences, and they believe God is at work leading them on their pilgrimage in the future.

They possess the same faith and hope of Abraham of old who followed God without a clear vision of precisely where and how God was leading his family (see Gen. 12:1-9). Although the pilgrimage of Abraham's family brought many bewildering experiences, the certainty of God's promise was crystal clear. Commitment to God's promise always enables a family to accept the experiences of life with gratitude and praise.

Peaceful contentment, rest, and assurance characterize the life-style of the family dedicated to the promises of God. Although Job suffered great personal and family stress, his peace and rest came to him through unwavering faith in the promises of God. Blessed peace and quiet contentment are reflected in the life-style of families whose faith rests in the promises of God.

Faithfulness to God's purposes is a constant challenge for the life-style of the family. The encouragement of Hebrews 13:5-8 is reassuring. "Be content with what you have; for he has said, 'I will never fail you nor forsake you.' Hence we can confidently say, 'The Lord is my helper, I will not be afraid; what can man do to me?' ... Jesus Christ is the same yesterday and today and for ever" (RSV).

Paul reminds believers that contentment is not only an ideal but is also reasonably possible (see Phil. 4:10-13). Families learn from experience how to be content in all of life's events. It is a witness for Christ's sake to be content and at peace with the difficult places in life as well as in the easier situations (see 2 Cor. 12:10).

Discipline, contentment, and peace create exciting expectancy because of what God is doing in the family. Authentic enthusiasm for life provides the life style of those families in Christ. Such enthusiasm does not need to be a flamboyant, reverberantly loud "praise the Lord" with every spoken sentence. But it affirms the sensitive awareness that God is near, even dwelling within, and this awareness leads to pure joy and honest excitement for living.

Any Christian family can blend its life-style so that it reflects the purposes and promises of God. The family needs only an openness to God's presence and to make a commitment to walk in his steps (see 1 Pet. 2:21). A family which adapts its daily life-style to the consistent, flexible, spirit and teachings of the Scriptures knows the joyful peace of accepting life's unfolding events with a sense of God's presence and praise. That acceptance of the circumstances of life forms a strong fiber in the total fabric of the ideal climate for *oikos* evangelism.

The Spirit of God abides in families of various sizes, types, and patterns. The ascended Christ desires intimate fellowship with every one of those Christian families. He desires to impart his Spirit and blessings in greater abundance. He wants greater involvement in the life of the family. He hopes families will feel a sense of excitement about what they are doing and becoming because of the power of God. God hopes the family will develop friendly, caring relationships with families who do not know the joy of Christ's presence. Then in the process of expressing love and care, members of the Christian family will share their living faith, abundant life, and the Christ who makes it all possible. Families witnessing to other families in deed and in word is *oikos* evangelism in action.

3.
Strategies for *Oikos* Evangelism

Current Research

Oikos evangelism has been discussed in terms of the Old and New Testaments and in terms of the climate necessary in family life for outreach to other families. The question still remains, How does *oikos* evangelism work in today's world? And does it work?

Recent Gallup polls, Church Growth studies of Billy Graham crusades and Here's Life America, studies of why people choose a church, and independent studies of Baptist leaders all lend credence to the fact that *oikos* evangelism is working today and that it does work. *Church Growth: America*, the bimonthly magazine of the Institute for American Church Growth,[21] carried an analysis of a recent Gallup poll showing:

1. Levels of belief and religious practice remain high.

2. Interest in religion is growing sharply.

3. The evangelical movement is having an increasingly powerful impact on religious life.

This kind of development provides a fertile field for *oikos* evangelism to be most effective. Win Arn of the Institute for American Church Growth says,

"There is great receptivity to the Gospel today that is unprecedented in the last 20 years."

Examples

The Billy Graham Crusades have had much success through the years and continue to be a major factor in evangelism today. One such crusade, the Greater Seattle Crusade, was described as, "the most exciting and successful U.S. Billy Graham Crusade in years."[22]

Church Growth: America conducted a research program one year after the Seattle Crusade to measure the level at which results were achieved in "making disciples and incorporating them into the body" (the church). The report is charted in detail in the January-February 1978 issue of *Church Growth: America*.[23] It reveals clearly the strong influence of the *oikos*, the web of friends and relatives, in effective evangelism follow-through.

The research revealed that almost eighty-three percent (82.8) of those who became members of a church as a result of the crusade were influenced to join the church they did because they already had a relative or friend (an *oikos* member) in that particular congregation. Win Arn, the author of the study, said, "Large numbers of persons (new Christians who are now in churches) were invited to the Crusade by friends or relatives. Following the decision, there was a natural 'door of entrance' into that same local church. This built-in follow-up, using established 'webs' or friends or relatives is particularly effective." This is a good example of *oikos* evangelism at work.

Arn continued, "Churches encouraging and equipping their members to reach the existing webs of friends or relatives, and then building them into the fellowship of the local church, will experience greatest results for their time and effort." This is undoubtedly true, whether it is a Graham Crusade, a local church revival, or week-by-week evangelism. A concerned, aware, trained *oikos* will increase evangelism effectiveness.

Surveys of follow-through after the "Here's Life America" efforts showed results quite different from the Graham Crusades. Virtually identical results were reported by two different surveys on the effectiveness of the "Here's Life America" or "I Found It" campaigns.

One was reported in *Eternity* magazine in the September 1977 issue and the other in *Church Growth: America* in the January-February 1978 issue. In both surveys, only three percent of those persons who claimed to have "found it" were ever incorporated into a church. Ninety-seven out of every one hundred who claimed to be professing Christ over the phone were never incorporated into a church.

These results demonstrate some of the problems encountered in evangelism that is impersonal and done between strangers. It demonstrates the 'non-*oikos*' approach to witnessing. It is contrary to New Testament evangelism which emphasizes that disciples are more than verbal converts (see Matt.). Participation in a church fellowship is important as an expression of one's faith in Jesus Christ.

Why People Join Churches

Many surveys have been conducted on the influences which lead people to a particular church. In a recent seminar at New Orleans Baptist Theological Seminary, Win Arn reported that out of eight thousand laypeople surveyed, friends or relatives (the *oikos*) were the most significant influence in 70 to 90 percent of the responses.

A similar survey of four hundred Baptist leaders revealed the following information. Questions and responses to the questions are listed.

1. Which part of the life and work of the church did you first have contact with?

>58% — Sunday School, Vacation Bible School, or a Bible Study Group
>
>14% — The worship services
>
>10% — Church Training
>
>8% — Music program
>
>6% — Revivals
>
>2% — Missions, benevolence, radio/television

Comment: Sunday School ministries, while not at the high level of the fifties, are still the strongest outreach tool in our churches. Bible Study is an effective way to "reach, teach, win, and develop" as one slogan of the Sunday School says.

2. Who was responsible for that initial contact?

>67% — A family member
>
>13% — Friends or neighbors
>
>11% — A Sunday School or VBS worker
>
>7% — Pastor or staff member

Comment: The top two responses which total 80 percent agree with other surveys on the effectiveness of the *oikos* in helping persons become a part of the local church. The low 11 percent Sunday School figure may indicate that many Sunday Schools do not have an active outreach program.

3. Who was most influential in your salvation process?

> 42% — Some family member
> 29% — Sunday School teacher or Vacation Bible School
> 18% — Pastor or other staff
> 11% — Friends/neighbors

Comment: Today the *oikos* system is still working effectively. A total of 53 percent were influenced by the *oikos* — family, friends, or neighbors. The impact of Bible teaching leaders is clearly evident in winning persons as well as in reaching them and teaching them. This question dealt with who was most influential rather than who triggered the final decision. This is why pastor and staff members ranked behind family members. In many cases the pastor and staff would probably rate much higher at the decision point.

While this survey was not intended to be a thorough scientific study, it did support and confirm other surveys that have been done on the effect of the *oikos* in evangelism. An example of how *oikos* works can be seen in the chart on pages 56 and 57. It points out some of the same conclusions that were seen in the survey.

Practical Projects

Thomas Edison was reported to have quipped on one occasion that genius was 10 percent inspiration and 90 percent perspiration. In a sense the same applies to our efforts to reach people for Christ. Ideas

EXAMPLE #1

Mrs. Priester (Enrolled in Sunday School in 1975)

└ Directly influenced her son and daughter-in-law

└ Her husband reached

└ Her sister reached

└ Sister's daughter reached

└ Granddaughter reached

└ Another daughter reached

└ Grandson reached

└ Reached Mr. and Mrs. Z. (neighbors)

└ Reached Mr. and Mrs. W. (neighbors)

└ Another neighbor now attending occasionally

EXAMPLE #2

Mrs. Albright joined three years ago.

└ Son and daughter-in-law reached

└ Daughter-in-law's mother reached

└ Granddaughter and her husband reached

└ Great grandson reached

└ } Several others in Mrs. Albright's extended family now being witnessed to and prayed for.

EXAMPLE #3

Family Active in Church

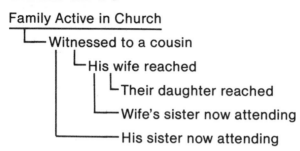

Witnessed to a cousin
His wife reached
Their daughter reached
Wife's sister now attending
His sister now attending

EXAMPLE #4

Mr. and Mrs. Winn – Church Members

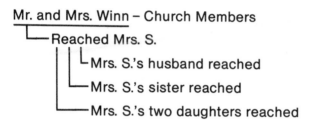

Reached Mrs. S.
Mrs. S.'s husband reached
Mrs. S.'s sister reached
Mrs. S.'s two daughters reached

THINK ABOUT THE WEBS OF OIKOS INFLUENCE
IN YOUR LIFE AND IN YOUR CHURCH

are useful and needed. New approaches are necessary. But when the final test of the effectiveness of any effort is made, it will be the results which determine its success. So it is with *oikos* evangelism. This book has sought to lend 10 percent inspiration through the discussion of *oikos* and the need for it. This section of the book is intended to give suggestions for the 90 percent more that must be done.

Suggestions will be given in the form of projects that can be attempted by the pastor, staff members, interested laypersons, or perhaps by a committee interested in reaching others with the gospel. Each project should be seen as simply an outline with suggestions. Individual churches should add to or delete from the outlines in order to meet felt needs.

Project 1—Your Family: A Witness for Christ

The purpose of this project is to involve church families in witnessing to other families who need the gospel. It will focus on *oikos* relationships as the sphere from which prospective families will be selected. This project can be initiated by the pastor, minister of outreach, family life minister, a committee such as the evangelism committee, or an interested couple in the church. The concept is simple in its scope.

What if every family in your church had a vision of reaching at least one other family for Christ during the year? The concept of one family reaching another family is not new. There are probably families in your church who are already doing this. Often the vision is blurred because many persons see evangelism as the pastor's job or something to be done only during revival meetings.

As a concerned leader in your church, you will seek to find other families who share your vision and begin with them as a core group. These families will maintain a close relationship within the core group as they seek to minister and witness to families in their own *oikos* relationships.

The first step is to recognize those persons who are within your *oikos*. Refer again to the diagram on page 19 which shows your *oikos* design. How many persons are there in your *oikos* who are lost? Identify them. How could an ongoing ministry to their needs open the way for you to witness to them about Jesus? These are the questions you must ask yourself and those who will join with you to reach their own *oikos* relationships.

If you are the initiator of this project, there are some important procedures to follow. Remember that this project should not be thrown open with a "ya'll come" invitation. Persons who participate in the project must have a conviction about leading others to Christ. They must be committed to working with a family for a long period of time and then to discipling them until they are able to lead others in their *oikos* to Christ.

Begin by thinking of others in the church who seem to have the same kind of interest in sharing their faith that you do. Take time to pray that God will give you the names of four to six families who share your vision of reaching others. Ask God to make you aware of families who already are involved in sharing their faith. Identify them by carefully watching to see who brings others to church with them to hear the gospel. Who are the families that openly talk about the victories they have won in sharing their faith?

Make a list of the names you have decided upon. List each family by name. Begin to pray for each family member by name. You should pray for each family and to ask that God make them even more sensitive to the need to reach others with the gospel. Since your next step will be to visit each family, it is important that God prepare the hearts of each family member.

After you have prayed for each family, visit them one by one. Share your vision and your awareness of their concern for reaching others. Ask the family to pray about becoming involved with a group of families in evangelistic outreach. Tell them that you will talk to them a little later after they have had time to seek God's will.

The church should be made aware of what is being done so that it can pray as a whole for those who are lost and for the ones who will be making an effort to begin to lead them to Christ. Simply ask the pastor to ask the church to pray for a group of families who are concerned about witnessing to those who need Christ. Avoid having the names of the participants made public.

Call or visit the families again to learn their decision. If a family cannot participate, thank them and ask them to pray for you and for the others. You may wish to find another family to replace them.

When at least four families have committed themselves to the project, schedule a meeting with the adults from the families. Older children can be included, or parents may wish to interpret the project to the children at a later time. You may wish to have this meeting in your home since you are taking responsibility for the group. If, however, you feel it would be better to meet at the church, then schedule time so that conflicts do not occur. Avoid publicizing the meeting except with involved persons.

You will want to avoid any criticism or idea that this group is somehow spiritually elite. If anyone asks about the group, be honest and explain that you are working with a group of families to win others to Christ and to help the church reach prospects it may not reach through its outreach program. It may be that the person asking really is interested in what is being done and may want to be part of such an endeavor. If his interest is strong, do not deny him opportunity to include his family in the group.

At the meeting in your home, discuss with the group something of the strategy for reaching others. Hand out blank sheets of paper and talk to the group about the idea of the *oikos*. Ask the group members to draw a picture similar to the diagram on page 19. You may wish to prepare a poster with the circles of influence already drawn so that each person will be able to see the pattern clearly.

After the circles are drawn ask each person to list members of his *oikos* in the circles. This exercise will be helpful in pointing out to each member his personal sphere of influence. Tell the group that this evangelistic strategy is largely based on the sphere of influence each person has.

Tell the group to think about the families who are represented in their circles. Ask them to identify at least one adult member who is lost. Then explain that the purpose of identifying those who are lost is so that you and your family can "adopt" that family on the basis of their needs.

The Christian family in the group will begin to be sensitive to the needs of the family they have chosen to adopt. Each person in the family should become sensitive to his counterpart in the lost family. Group members should explain carefully the design of the strategy to their children who are Christians.

Youth and older children who are Christians can have an active part in witnessing to the lost family. Through their own contacts with their peers in the lost family, they will be able to cultivate friendships and genuine relationships which will be valuable foundations from which to begin to share Christ.

Explain what it means to be sensitive to needs. Each family will have needs in certain areas. They may have physical needs. They may need help with food or medical assistance. Children in the Christian family can be sensitive to these kinds of needs which are sometimes reflected in the children in the lost family. Does the family have adequate clothing? Do they have heat for the winter? These are the kinds of needs that must be met immediately.

Another kind of need is often caused by some crisis that has occurred. Moving to another community, loss of jobs, extreme sickness, death, divorce, and other related traumas are crises that can tax the family heavily. The Christian family will want to be first on the scene if there is a death or sickness in the adopted family.

A third area of need is more complex. It is spiritual in nature. Persons in the family may not only be lost but actually confused about religious beliefs. They may be caught up in some kind of cultic belief, or influenced by some sect which has confused them about the gospel. It may be that they have ruled out religion as a part of their lives. Their religion may be secularism, materialism, or some other philosophy which reflects their need for Christ.

Be sure to be sensitive to whatever need the lost family has. Many times giving a cup of cold water is important and necessary before sharing your faith can be effective. Talk together in family discussion about these kinds of needs. Share how each family member can help in the ministry to needs. Remember to keep confidential any sharing that takes place in family discussions. Avoid saying anything in the presence of younger family members that you do not want repeated to the family to whom you are seeking to minister.

Stress the importance of the privacy of the family you are seeking to win. They have a right to their privacy, and you must not do anything that would invade their privacy. Make sure that children understand this completely. Your ministry to their needs must be a natural and caring ministry. You must not be guilty of using the family as only a project for witnessing. Genuine caring will open the doors for sharing.

When a ministry to the lost family has been initiated, take the time necessary to clarify that your concern comes from your relationship with Jesus Christ. Just as you are concerned about the need they are experiencing, Jesus also is concerned — not only about the current stress but about their spiritual needs as well.

Often in times of need people become more receptive to the gospel. The chart below indicates some of the times when people listen more attentively to the gospel message. Remember, do not take

RECEPTIVITY RATING CHART

The following chart shows the influence that an event in a family's life can have on their willingness to listen to the gospel. The events are listed in an approximate order of their importance. The chart is adapted from a chart by W. Charles Arn.

100
DEATH OF A SPOUSE

73
DIVORCE

63
DEATH OF A FAMILY MEMBER

53
PERSONAL INJURY OR ILLNESS

50
MARRIAGE

44
CHANGE IN FAMILY MEMBER'S HEALTH

39
ADDITION TO FAMILY

31
MORTGAGE OR LOAN OVER $10,000

30
FORECLOSURE OF MORTGAGE OR LOAN

26
SPOUSE STARTS WORK

23
TROUBLE WITH BOSS

20
CHANGE IN RESIDENCE

17
EASTER SEASON

12
CHRISTMAS SEASON

advantage of a person's misfortune or need to satisfy your zeal for sharing the gospel. It may be that you will make them more resistant to the gospel. They may blame God for what has happened. Rather, take time to help them and share your faith naturally with them. Of course, you and your family will be the best judge of such times. If you establish the kind of relationship with the lost family that is conducive to sharing your faith, usually there will be no difficulties in this area.

As you minister to needs, you will have the opportunity to share your faith. Each family in the core group should sit down with family members and explore the kinds of things that the family has to share. Sitting down together as a family and discovering exactly what your family has to share can be vital in learning to share your faith with other families. Ask these questions of your family. What makes our family unique? What special gift do we have that can be shared with another family? What special resources does our Christian family have that may not be present in a non-Christian family? What is our Christian family testimony?

The following suggestions can be used to help your family determine exactly what you have to share with lost families. Ask your family to join you in a time of sharing when the entire family can meet together, share ideas, and discuss problems.

• Read 2 Timothy 1:5. Talk about how Timothy's family had shared their faith in Christ from one generation to the next. Discuss how important it is for parents to share their faith in Christ with their children. Read Matthew 28:19-20 and discuss how Jesus told us to share our faith.

• Ask your family to pray with you about being a witness in your community. Ask God to lead your family discussion.

• Ask, Does our family have anything special to share with people outside our family? What does it mean to be a Christian? What makes a Christian family like ours different from other families? What do family Bible study and worship mean to our family? What does regular attendance at church mean to our family? Has God blessed our family in a special way recently? As Christians do we take opportunities to minister to others who are in need?

• Write down key words and phrases which describe the unique nature of your Christian family. Ask each family member to contribute to the list.

• Ask, What special resources does our family have? List your Bibles, prayers, church, Christian friends and relatives as starters. Talk about how much God has blessed your family and how much you can share with other families who are not Christian.

• Close by praying for the family you have chosen to minister to. Ask God to allow your family to share his love with them.

Sharing a Verbal Witness

As you minister to the family you have chosen, the time will come when you can share the why of your ministry. You will be able to share a verbal witness. Since you have been ministering on the basis of their needs, your witnessing opportunities may come as a direct result of this ministry or because you have shown such an interest in the family. When the opportunity for witnessing does come, be sure to remember some essentials.

Sometimes you may sense that the time is not right for a verbal witness. Using a tract such as "How to Have a Full and Meaningful Life" or perhaps one of the salvation tracts from the Choice Creation Tract series[24] may be the best approach. The tract might be included with a gift, left as a follow-up of a visit, or included in a note of interest, love, and concern.

When the time is right for a verbal witness, you will want to share your faith so that the other person both understands and shows continued interest in what you are saying. As we minister to needs and as we confront persons with the gospel, we need to understand the value of speaking under the right circumstances. Care in not embarrassing the other person will keep the door open for your witness.

As you share, do not give the impression that you have selected that family so that you can enroll them in Sunday School or so that you will have someone to witness to. Give the correct impression. You care about them as persons. Share from your own personal life. Tell what Christ has done for you and for your family. Emphasize the joy that is yours by knowing Christ.

Often the verbal encounter will be on a one-to-one basis with the father witnessing to the father of the other family, the mother of the Christian family witnessing to the mother of the other family, and so on. There are other approaches that can be used as well.

The two families may be together, with one person taking the lead in witnessing while others support. Or one person may witness to each member of the other family, either individually or as a family group. Use the approach that is best for your own family group, but make the decision together as a family. Even if one person is selected to witness verbally, involve other family members in intercessory prayer so that the entire family becomes involved.

Some people respond to the gospel almost immediately. With others it takes much longer. Unfortunately, some might not ever say yes to Christ. We must be willing to offer the gospel message to that person both as it is lived out in our lives and in verbal form and to keep doing it that he might have the opportunity to invite Christ into his life.

Making Your Home a Witness Center

In the family discussion you should have talked about ways to make your home available as a witnessing center. Following are a few ways your home can serve as a witnessing center. Study the list and select those ways your family can witness best. You will probably think of other ways your home can become a witnessing center. Be careful to avoid situations in which your guests are made to feel like they are a captive audience or that they are on display.

• Host a Bible study or Christian growth group. If no one in your family feels led to conduct the study, invite someone to lead it for you and let your family serve as host. Invite several Christian friends or community members as well as the lost family you are seeking to win. This is an ideal way to expose them to the gospel.

• Invite neighbors to a cookout with other Christian friends. This will help to expose the lost family to Christian related activities. Your family will be able to show your guests that Christians know how to laugh and enjoy life.

• Open your home to clubs and other groups.

Groups for children, youth, and adults, such as mission organizations, scouts, campus organizations, and business-professional clubs often need places to meet or would welcome a change of scenery. Invite the lost family to come or to let their children participate.

• Be a good neighbor. If the lost family is your neighbor, be sensitive to what happens next door. Watch out for their home when they are away. Look for ways to work together on projects, and so forth.

• Other ideas include providing chauffeur service, babysitting, shopping for the lost family when someone is ill, and so forth. What are some other ways that you can open your home to the family you are seeking to witness to?

Your family can find a new meaning in the word *friend*. As you witness to the lost family, your will not only be sensitive to their needs and minister to them but you will also have opportunity to lead them to life eternal and to help them relate to their own *oikos*.

As you help to disciple the family once a decision has been made, remember to keep the relationship alive and open. Do not discard them once a positive decision has been made. Involve the persons or the entire family in your church and provide support so that they can continue the pilgrimage they have started. Also, find ways to maintain contact with those whose decision might be negative.

Utilize some of the resources that are available for personal discipleship. Use something like the *Survival Kit for New Christians*, Sunday School materials, materials available from denominational publishing houses, and other materials available.

It often has been said that evangelism is not complete until the one who has found Christ as Savior shares his faith with someone else. When a family who is lost makes a decision for Christ as a result of your family's witness, you will experience a great deal of personal joy. But that joy will be greater as you see the new family in Christ begin to witness to other families they know. If this should happen with each Christian family, very soon our world could be won to Christ.

Project 2—Leading Your Child to Christ

One of life's greatest joys is that of leading your child to faith in Jesus Christ. But most parents do not experience that joy. There are many reasons why this is so.

Many parents feel unqualified. Some treat the salvation experience as they would treat an item that is in need of repair. If their car or household appliance is broken, they take it to an expert who fixes it. Since the pastor is often viewed as the expert on religious matters, why not take the child to him?

A pastor or staff member should recognize that many parents would rather carry their children to the pastor's study for counseling than to go through the process themselves. For years this has been the assumed procedure on the part of many parents.

Some parents may feel they do not know what to say to the child. He may ask questions they are not sure they can answer. Many church members today are reflecting their own need for more Bible study if this is the reason they give.

Other parents may feel their child will not listen to them if they talk to the child about his salvation experience. This reason may indicate that the parent and the child need help in learning to communicate with one another. This can develop into a serious problem in later years if left unresolved.

There are many other reasons why parents do not share their faith with their children. Many of these reasons reflect the need for parents to understand the basic principles of *oikos* evangelism. One principle that is basic is the sharing of the faith from one generation to another (see Deut. 6:20-25).

There are many books available on the subject of leading children to Christ. It is outside the scope of this book to discuss this subject in detail. However, this project is suggested to help pastors and staff members equip parents to lead their children to Christ. The actual content of the project must be left up to the pastor or staff members and the parents since needs vary and since the discussion needs to be open to questions that may be raised. Suggestions will be given to guide the discussion.

This project suggests a method that can be used with parents who sense that their child is ready to begin talking about a decision for Christ or for those parents who have already been questioned by their child about salvation. This project can be utilized with one couple or with as many parents as seems appropriate. A pastor or staff member may wish to schedule the project only when parents ask for it or as a regular course for parents offered two or three times a year.

The format of the project must be a little different from the usual kinds of courses or projects that are open for church members. Try to hold the meeting with parents in a place that is quiet and relaxed and where informal discussion can take place. Avoid the temptation to lecture during the conference with parents. This will enable discussion to take place and help parents deal with any questions that need detailed answers.

Be sure to schedule enough time for the conference. You will probably need four to six times together to cover the material adequately. Do not drag the meeting along, however, but try to meet the needs that are voiced and take time to do so.

Before you attempt to lead parents in this project you should acquaint yourself afresh with the materials that have been written on the subject. A partial list might include: *A Theology for Children* by William L. Hendricks; *Children and Conversion* edited by Clifford Ingle; *When Can A Child Believe* by Eugene Chamberlain; and *Children and the Christian Faith* by Cos H. Davis. These books are helpful for a proper understanding of the salvation experience and children. Other materials that deal with conversion and children can be helpful.

Begin the meeting by having each parent introduce himself and call the name of the child who is concerned about making a decision for Christ. Have a time of prayer and pray for each family and the child who is involved.

Discuss the concept of *oikos* with the parents. Be sure to include the idea that each parent is responsible for sharing Christ with his family members. Parallel today's family with the family of the Old Testament. Note the differences but pay close attention to what God commanded Old Testament families to do in regard to sharing their faith with their children. Use Deuteronomy 6:4-7, 20-25 as a springboard for discussion.

You may wish to expand the discussion to include something of the parent's responsiblity for religious training in the home. Ask parents to suggest ways religious awareness is communicated to children. Ask a parent in the group who has been successful in family worship and Bible study to share with the group.

Discuss the concept of lostness. Help parents understand that a child's concept of being lost is different from that of an adult. Give some examples that you as pastor have noted of how children verbalize lostness. Ask parents to think carefully about conversations they have had with their children to discover if their child has expressed any such feelings.

Talk about some of the signs that children exhibit that may indicate they are interested in making a decision for Christ. Help the group to discover which signs are which. It may be that the child is responding to influences other than the Holy Spirit. Point out to the parents that as adults we often want to read into the child's response more than is there. Help the group understand how a child might communicate his faith in Christ.

Help parents understand that religious language can sometimes be confusing. Give examples of the group of words we use only at church. Ask the group to discover words that mean the same thing but communicate in everyday English. Encourage parents to use understandable words with their children.

Provide some concrete suggestions to the parents about what to say to the child about becoming a Christian. You may wish to use section three in Cos Davis's book, *Children and the Christian Faith.* This section, "Teaching the Faith," is intended for use by the parents in the home. Enough copies should be available for parents to borrow. You may wish to use ideas from Gene Chamberlain's book, *When Can a Child Believe?* Chapter six will be helpful.

Encourage parents to keep in touch with you and to

let you know what progress is being made with their children. This will continue dialogue and make you available in case questions arise which did not occur in the group discussion. Provide support to the parents through prayer and through your continued interest in the families. You may even wish to preach a sermon series on *oikos* evangelism which will provide extra support for family evangelism.

Project 3—Bible Studies in Homes

An ongoing project that can be started is Bible study groups in homes and by neighborhoods. Many churches have reported successes with persons receiving Christ as Savior and new members being added to Sunday School rolls through such groups.

One church in Louisiana has developed a formal plan for the development of home Bible study groups.[25] This suggestion is based on that plan and is compatible with weektime Bible study patterns and fellowship Bible classes.

Begin by considering families who might be willing to participate in the project by opening their homes for the study. These families will serve as hosts for the study groups and must be willing to do so on a continuing basis.

You may wish to begin with only three or four families at first. Ask the families involved to select a time during the week that is most convenient for them. Since the study will take place in their homes, every effort needs to be made to fit the study to their schedule of activities. It would be helpful to avoid Wednesday night so that family members would be free to attend prayer meeting and other mid-week church activities. This could eliminate any criticism of the groups for creating a conflict with regular church meetings and functions.

Home Bible study teachers should be elected by the church. They could be recommended by the Sunday School director to the nominating committee just as Sunday School teachers are. If it seems desirable, the host family might participate in the teaching responsibilities.

An outreach leader may be elected by the church for each Bible study group. This person will assist the host family in enlisting families and by keeping records, enrollment, and making contacts. The outreach leader should work closely with the host family to secure the names of neighbors, relatives, and others in the *oikos* of the host family and participants.

There is no hard and fast rule for group size. However, the membership goal of the home Bible study probably should be approximately fifteen. This might include a nucleus of six or eight church members who wish to participate. The rest should be prospects or non-members. You will have to establish the proper ratio for each group on the basis of participation and interest.

The church should also elect a leader to be responsible for home Bible studies in the same way other department directors are chosen. This person would be in charge of administering several home Bible study groups just as a department director administers several classes in the regular Sunday School departments. Regular planning meetings should be held with other elected leaders in order to work out any problem areas and to make plans for each session.

Good literature is available for use by home Bible study groups. For example, the Sunday School Board of the Southern Baptist Convention publishes a number of items that are useful in this project. The curriculum for these Bible study groups might include the Bible Book

Series if your church uses Convention Uniform or Life
and Work Series in the regular Sunday School program.
The Bible Book Series is designed to go through the
Bible in a systematic way and is excellent for home Bible
studies. Also, Vacation Bible School materials for adults,
Bible Study Course books, and undated Bible study materials are available. January Bible Study materials are
good sources as are materials from the Church Study
Course series. Some groups might prefer to study materials on doctrine published by the Church Training Department. Be creative in your selections.

The length of the study will depend on the group
and its needs. A good rule of thumb is to let the group
study together for thirteen weeks. During and following
this period, the members of the home Bible study group
who are not in regular Sunday Bible study should be encouraged to move into the regular Sunday School structure.

Project 4—Family Outreach During Revival

Many churches regularly schedule revival efforts
during the year. For many churches this represents the
sole, major effort at evangelistic outreach. Yet, some
churches make little or no effort to insure that the revival will be successful. Very little is done in outreach
and the discovery of prospects for the revival. Hence,
the evangelistic revival often is focused more toward
church members than toward lost persons.

This project is intended to help discover prospects
and to mobilize the membership so that lost persons will
be present in the revival services. As with the other projects listed, the pastor and staff members should take the
lead in the implementation of this project.

Begin at least two or three months before the revival services are to take place. Have cards printed similar to the one shown below. Print enough to place several in each pew rack and to have to hand out to persons who attend worship services. You will need to do this early in case it takes time to get the cards back from the printer. You will need the cards back from the printer at least one month before the revival is to begin.

At least six weeks before the revival is to begin, announce to the congregation that a project to discover prospects is going to be attempted in addition to the cottage prayer meetings and other preparatory efforts you are making for the revival. Tell the church that the project will begin in two weeks. Each service until then, remind the church that something special will happen.

On the Sunday morning that will begin the project, check to see that prospect cards are in the pews and that

PROSPECT CARD

I Know A Prospect

Name _____

Address_____

Phone_____

Relationship _____

Additional Information_____

_____

ushers have an ample supply. Arrange the format for the service so that time will be reserved to begin the project. It probably will take from ten to fifteen minutes. Do not add on this project at the end of the service because it may make some people not want to participate if the service is prolonged.

Tell the congregation that the church is seeking to discover prospects for the revival crusade. Ask each member to take a prospect card from his pew or ask the ushers to hand each person a card.

Talk for a couple of minutes about the importance of having lost persons in the revival services and indicate to the congregation how these lost persons often go overlooked because we do not actively seek to involve them in the services of our churches. Explain that these lost persons are part of our *oikos* and that each person probably has lost persons in his *oikos* system.

Tell the church that you would like for each member to list on the prospect card the name of one person who is lost. If possible also list the address and phone number of that person. The card will have room on it for comments about the person. He may travel and be hard to contact or he may work at night. These kinds of comments should be placed on the card.

Help members identify their *oikos* by suggesting the kinds of people who make up an *oikos* system. Begin with the immediate family. Are there lost persons in the immediate family (father, mother, son, daughter, husband, wife, and so on)? Move to the larger or extended family. Are there lost grandparents, aunts, uncles, or cousins? Ask that their names be listed on a prospect card. Then move to friends, neighbors, working relationships, and so on. Follow as closely as possible the structure of the *oikos* as shown in the diagram on page 19. Having copies of the diagram available will make the explanation of *oikos* easier.

Thank church members for taking the time to list the ones in their *oikos* who are lost. Ask them to begin to pray for the ones they have listed. Ask the ushers to collect the prospect cards from the members.

During the week place each card in an envelope and place them in categories: children, youth, adults, senior adults. On the next Sunday morning review with the church the fact that many cards were turned in. Thank them for their response. Have the cards placed on the altar or somewhere near the pulpit so that members can see them.

Ask members to come to the front and choose an envelope from the category with which they would like to work. They will not be able to read the names of the person on the prospect cards since they will be in plain envelopes. They will only see the categories at the time of card selection.

When members return to their seats, ask them to take the prospect card from the envelope and look at the name of the person they have chosen to seek to enlist for the revival. Ask members to begin to pray for the person listed on the card and to pray for that person each day. Have a few moments of silent prayer and then a prayer of dedication for the work that will be done.

Ask members to contact the person listed on the card three or four times before the revival is to be held and to invite the person to attend. Ask members to make a special effort to enlist the person for the revival effort and to keep the person in prayer all through the revival time.

Members should be given cards to send to the person who is a prospect. These postcards are not expensive and will make it easier for members to drop the prospect a note inviting him to attend the revival. Ask members to volunteer to provide transportation to the revival for their prospect if necessary.

This project can be very helpful in discovering prospects at revival time, but it is also a good discipline to help members become more sensitive to the lost persons in their *oikos* system. If this project is taken seriously by members, the revival effort will be more of a success in terms of lost persons who come to hear the gospel.

Project 5—Family Worship and Bible Study

A helpful project that centers on the home and family worship can be built around the training module intitled *How to Lead Your Family in Worship and Bible Study*. Parents will receive practical help in developing their skills for spiritual experiences together at home. Parents will learn how to plan and conduct a family together time one evening each week. The evening activities will focus on Bible study, worship, and family fun in which each member of the family can be meaningfully involved. The module can be secured from Materials Services, Baptist Sunday School Board, 127 Ninth Avenue North, Nashville, Tennessee 37234.

Other Projects

Listed below are several other strategy starters. These are ideas that can be used to design your own project. Use these ideas as a springboard for projects which can be done in Sunday School departments, as a project of the evangelism committee, or by a group of interested laypersons.

• Good neighbor visitation—If your community is one that has a large turnover of new persons, this project can be of help. You may wish to ask persons in a certain neighborhood to agree to visit newcomers or prospects. Help the newcomer get acquainted with his neighbors and his new town. Be his spiritual "Welcome Wagon" by carrying a bulletin, Sunday School literature, a letter from the pastor, and other items to him. Invite the new family members to church and offer to provide transportation or to meet them there.

• Family Outreach Day—Have a Sunday School emphasis on families. Ask families to sit together in worship service and recognize each family who brings a guest family from their *oikos* system.

• Recreation events—Schedule a churchwide picnic for Independence Day or some other time. Invite church members to bring neighbors and friends. Have singing and a brief praise time together.

• Lay Evangelism Schools—Plan a Lay Evangelism School for your church. Complete plans can be obtained from your state evangelism office or by writing the Evangelism Section of the Home Mission Board, Atlanta, Georgia. Emphasis should be placed on three areas of planning:

1. Pre-enroll as many parents as possible. This will aid parents in the process of sharing their faith with their children.

2. Study carefully all older children and youth Sunday School rolls for unsaved prospects. Contact their parents and urge them to enroll in the school.

Be sure to include the names of the lost youth and children in the list of persons to be visited on witnessing nights.

3. Ask the teacher to make specific suggestions for witnessing to family members.

• Morning coffees—Several homemakers may be interested in opening their homes for refreshments and a brief Bible study and period of personal testimony and discussion. Neighbors and friends along with church members could be invited to attend.

• Sports time out—Invite neighboring families into your home to watch a sporting event on television. Be sure to provide activities for those family members who are not interested in sporting events. Plan a time of Christian sharing and fellowship for the entire group.

• Backyard Bible Clubs—Materials for these clubs can be found at Baptist Book Stores and other religious book stores. Children from the neighborhood should be encouraged to attend. Follow-up with the parents who are prospects is essential.

The best ideas for you and for your church will be those which you plan carefully. The goal of any of these projects is that of helping church members become more aware of their *oikos* and more concerned about the lost and needy persons in it. The fact is that *Oikos* evangelism works. It worked in New Testament times, and it can work today. "What must I do to be saved?" was not only the cry of a jailer, but it is the cry of homemakers, youth, members of families, friends, and neighbors today. The Bible gives the results of *oikos* evangelism. "Believe in the Lord Jesus, and you shall be saved, you and your *oikos*."

Notes

1. Michael Green, *Evangelism in the Early Church* (Grand Rapids: Eerdmans Publishing Co., 1975), p. 210.

2. Ibid.

3. Hans Walter Wolff, *Anthropology of the Old Testament* (Philadelphia: Fortress Press, 1974), p. 215.

4. Ibid.

5. Green, p. 210.

6. James Hastings, *Dictionary of the New Testament* (Grand Rapids: Baker Book House, 1975), Vol. 1, p. 752.

7. Tom Wolf, "Oikos Evangelism," *Church Growth: America* (January-February 1978), p. 11.

8. Ibid., p. 12.

9. Ibid., p. 13.

10. Oscar E. Feucht, ed., *Family Relationships and the Church* (Saint Louis: Concordia Publishing House, 1970), p. 28.

11. Edith Deen, *Family Living in the Bible* (New York: Harper and Row, 1963), p. 12.

12. Ibid., p. 41.

13. Oscar E. Feucht, ed., *Helping Families Through the Church* (Saint Louis: Concordia Publishing House, 1957), pp. 103-104.

14. Jack R. Taylor, *One Home Under God* (Nashville: Broadman Press, 1974), pp. 96-97.

15. Feucht, *Helping Families*, p. 84.

16. Gallup Poll, Religion in America, 1979-80.

17. Feucht, *Helping Families*, p. 34.

18. Ibid., p. 93.

19. Ibid., pp. 44-46.

20. Larry Christensen, *The Christian Family* (Minneapolis:

Bethany Fellowship, Inc., 1970), p. 65.

21. *Church Growth: America* (March-April 1978).

22. *Decision Magazine* (August 1976).

23. *Church Growth: America* (March-April 1978).

24. Choice Creation Tracts are available from Baptist Sunday School Board, 127 Ninth Avenue North, Nashville, Tennessee 37234.

25. Emmanuel Baptist Church, Ruston, Louisiana.

Bibliography

Arn, Win. "Evangelism—the Bottom Line," *Church Growth: America*. Pasadena: Institute for American Church Growth, January-February 1978.

Arn, Win. "The Pendulum Swings," *Church Growth: America*. Pasadena: Institute for American Church Growth, March-April 1978.

Brown, Colin. *The New International Dictionary of New Testament Theology*, Vol. 2. Grand Rapids: Zondervan, 1976.

Christensen, Larry. *The Christian Family*. Minneapolis: Bethany Fellowship, Inc., 1970.

Deen, Edith. *Family Living in the Bible*. New York: Harper and Row, 1963.

Feucht, Oscar E., ed. *Family Relationships and the Church*. Saint Louis: Concordia Publishing House, 1970.

Feucht, Oscar E., ed. *Helping Families Through the Church*. Saint Louis: Concordia Publishing House, 1957.

Green, Michael. *Evangelism in the Early Church*. Grand Rapids: Eerdmans Publishing Co., 1970.

Hastings, James. *Dictionary of the New Testament*, Vol. 1. Grand Rapids: Baker Book House, 1973.

Lenski, Richard. *Interpretation of the Acts of the Apostles*. Minneapolis: Augsburg, 1961.

McDill, Wayne. *Making Friends for Christ*. Nashville: Broadman Press, 1979.

Neil, William. "Acts of the Apostles," *New Century Bible*. London: Oliphants, 1973.

Olthius, James. *I Pledge My Troth*. New York: Harper and Row, 1975.

Richards, Lawrence. *A Theology of Christian Education*. Grand Rapids: Zondervan, 1975.

Taylor, Jack R. *One Home Under God*. Nashville: Broadman Press, 1974.

Wolf, Tom. "Oikos Evangelism," *Church Growth: America*. Pasadena: Institute for American Church Growth, January-February 1978.

Wolff, Hans Walter. *Anthropology of the Old Testament*. Philadelphia: Fortress Press, 1974.

Appendix

OIKOS ACTIONS AND IDEAS

Project
Idea or Activity_____
What we hope to achieve (Goal)_____
_____

STEP BY STEP STRATEGY: (What we'll need to get ready to start this *oikos* activity)

	Person/Group Responsible	Date to be Completed	Resources Needed
1.			
2.			
3.			
4.			
5.			

This worksheet may be reproduced for use by individuals or groups planning *oikos* activities.

OIKOS PROSPECT SEARCH FORM

Your Name_____

Address_____

Phone _____

Use this form to list your unsaved family members, friends, and associates. The various categories are simply to help you recall them. Give name, address, approximate age, and any other information you feel would be helpful. This information will be helpful to the pastor and other church leaders as they join you in prayer for those you list and as they help you enlist or win them. Write on the back of the sheet if more space is needed.

NEIGHBORS (Nearby) (Distant)

_____
_____
_____
_____

FAMILY WITH A NEW BABY

_____
_____
_____
_____

NEWCOMER TO THE COMMUNITY

_____
_____
_____

RELATIVES

_____
_____
_____

CLOSE PERSONAL FRIENDS

_____

_____

_____

PERSONS ILL OR IN A CRISIS

_____

_____

_____

HOBBY, HUNTING, & FISHING FRIENDS

_____

_____

_____

VOCATIONAL ASSOCIATES

_____

_____

_____

CONTACTS IN ORGANIZATIONS OR CLUBS

_____

_____

_____

NEW HOMES AND THOSE BUILDING OR BUYING

_____

_____

_____

NOTE: This _Oikos_ Prospect Search Form may be used with any church member group but it is especially useful in helping new Christians and new church members identify unsaved persons in their _oikos_.